No One Dies

at the
Au Bon Pain

Doug Holder

sunnyoutside
Somerville,
Massachusetts

Acknowledgments

Thanks is due to the following publications in which some of these poems originally appeared: *sub-TERRAIN*, *Ibbetson Street*, *The Boston Poet*, *Poesy*, *Spare Change News*, *PLAZM*, and *Carbon 14*.

Copyright 2007 Doug Holder.

Original artwork by Ed Herrera.
Copyright 2007 sunnyoutside.

All rights reserved.
Printed in the United States of America.

ISBN-13: 978-1-934513-00-2
ISBN-10: 1-934513-00-8

sunnyoutside
P.O. Box 441429
Somerville, MA 02144
USA
www.sunnyoutside.com

Edition of 150.

Table of Contents

No One Dies at the Au Bon Pain	5
A Reflection of Myself in Her Eyes	6
Vacation from Selfhood	7
Flux	8
I Am Not Afraid of Bones	9
Am I a Man of Bone or Flesh?	10
An Old Black Man Laughing at Me	11
Just Before...	12
Why Did He Leave Her?	13
The Atrium at the Boston Public Library	14
Public Restrooms	16
A Tear from a Glass Eye	18
All This Rain	19
Before I Go...	20
Colonoscopy	21
Boston Common: 1973	22
My Life: In Contrast with Others	24
Glaucoma	25

No One Dies at the Au Bon Pain

As far as I can see
no one has crumpled
into the recesses
of their daily rag.
No one is supine
in wide-eyed wonderment
staring at the abyss.
The febrile cacophony
goes on,
and the old man struggles
to his table
gripping his cane
and routine
almost breathless….
The mist rises from his cup
and the headlines slap him to
full consciousness.
The chess players still
lust for their checkmates
and for this day
all is well
the next
one never
can tell.

A Reflection of Myself in Her Eyes

Perhaps it is not
her I love.
Not her wistful
gray/blue eyes
but what they reflect—
some dusted, discarded
image of myself
that reappears
to my stunned
surprise.

Perhaps
it is not her many virtues
that I see,
but that younger
hopeful
reflection of
Me.

Vacation from Selfhood

Oh
the bliss
of the blank slate.
When "nothing"
crosses the mind's portals
much more
than once.
That identity
that clings
like a
cheap suit
releases your
body
from its
musty grip.
The constant
rehash,
the replay
lost in
an amorphous
ether.
Asleep…
awake…
neither?

Flux

It's no use
it all slips
from your greased palm.
So solid today
a torrent of fluid
the next.
The tug of heartstrings
now the nag
of tired obligation…
And ye of little
faith—
who wore such
a loud creed
on your sleeve,
tell me
with a
straight face
that you won't
leave.

I Am Not Afraid of Bones

I am not afraid of bones.
I trace them
through a façade of flesh.
My tongue
is often crowned,
tipped with
marrow.
And there
is always
the joke
of a skeleton
under the myth
of the most beautiful woman.

Bones—
they are what
make us
most human.

Am I a Man of Bone or Flesh?

I am more
than stick
or bone,
an empty
coat rack
for no one's
home.

Can you still
feel my supple flesh,
like a fruit's
skin blushing
with ripeness?

And yes
I know
where I
stand,
and the bone
lays perilously close
to the flesh of my hand—

still I am more
than brittle bone,
the cold
unfeeling face
of glacial stone.

An Old Black Man Laughing at Me

As I passed him
I heard the guttural laugh
the knee slapping—
the astringent
mixture of the hilarious
and sinister.
We were partners of sorts
with no formal introduction.
He knew what
my sorry ass had been up to.
How I made
that motherfuckin' mole hill
into a mountain.
And I better
move my bone-ugly hide—
and save
that chicken-shit walk,
that head-tilting attitude
for someone who hasn't
seen it before,
and has time
to give
a
good
God
Damn.

Just Before...

Just before the fifth gin and tonic
and lime,
when fragments are put in a narrative line,
when the tremor in my hand
is still for a short time,
when all these stumblebums
are friends of mine,
wouldn't that fifth drink
be a bloody crime?

Why Did He Leave Her?

Because of the terminal
certainty of the itinerary—
his course redlined
with an actuary's passionless
calculation,
a replay of his father's descent.

And with her—
so young,
he reinvented his flame
but of course
the outcome
is always
the same.

The Atrium at the Boston Public Library

I sit in limbo
looking at the perpetual
ejaculation of
the fountain
under a shock
of blue sky,
in a gap
between wings—
old and new.
A pause from
the confluence
of past and present,
watching the ivy
grip on the
old edifice.
The clouds
drift
shadows flit on the pavement.

Still I know
I can only
walk from old to new,
that the brittle tomes
will decay.
So I
will sit
and pause
for just
this day.

Public Restrooms

I once viewed them as religious places,
men with their backs to me
in front of urinals
hands clasped together
at their crotch
as if in prayer.

Facing their Wailing Wall
reading the graffiti
cryptic messages
cries of urgency
anger, bitter humor
a standing chant
a prayer for the
common man,
as the vile within comes out
in a steady stream
and then a slow trickle.

I love the intimacy
of the stall.
I see only the feet
of my fellow congregants,
alone with myself
and my maker—
my
silent meditation.

The mirror—
the fluorescent
light, divine
and radiant,
I confess
my flaws
in full, merciless view
and wash my
self in
holy
tap water.

A Tear from a Glass Eye

Perhaps it is better
that I view this as an absurdity
or a mere condensation
on an inanimate
piece of quartz.
I should
come up
with
another rational
explanation
for another drop
in the bucket and
realize
it's just a

dreamer's
cry in the dark.

I chuckle
and close its case
and wipe
the dampness
from my cheek.

All This Rain

And when will it end?
A week of lamenting
rain.

A rain—
not unlike
a dull,
enduring
pain.

A spectral tapping
on the roof,
wanting an in…

ghosts…
bloodless pricks
on my thin skin
reminding me of
where I've been.

Before I Go...

And will
there be a
place with a delicious
hush...
a lap in the land
where I can finally rest
my riotous head?
And there
will be no need to
charge the wind—
I will let it
brush and
replenish my
barren cheek.

Will I accept
the ocean's tide
the high and low
the ebb and flow

before I go?

Colonoscopy

In the funeral parlor bathroom
I thought
odd
how the light
seems to divinely illuminate me
through the stained glass window
as if I was part of a purifying ritual.

I strained and strained
and wondered about
that test
and how long
I have before
that dreaded
rest.

Boston Common: 1973

Sitting—
amidst the angry
invective
of the soap box preachers—
burnt out
by the fire and brimstone
carried by
a hot September breeze.

I am only a freshman...
fleeing
Boston University
for the nameless riot,
wondering if the man next to me
with the broken posture
and the shopworn suit,
his dreams
that hit the crapper
years ago—
will this
be me?

My carefully prepared face
washed away
with the press
of all this strange
sweaty, flesh.
The familial wisdom
passed on to me
like some precious heirloom—
useless, ludicrous
in this new light.
And my questions
float unanswered.
The city's febrile pulse unabated—

I wilt in
leafy shadows.

My Life: In Contrast with Others

There is no need for comparison.
Nor is their time.
What I wanted before
has been rendered to caricature.
The phantoms that pull at me
I will never clearly see—

the only contrast
will be that short
tenuous last breath
that will surely be
the death

of me.

Glaucoma

And how those angelic halos
around the streetlights
change
to an homage of
nefarious intent.

The pressure
the threat
builds
and those images
of her smile,

the Maine coast,
the surf jumping
the rocks
as its mussels maintain
a tight grip.

And I don't see
in wanton gulps
but I sip
baby

I sip.

Biography

Doug Holder was born in Manhattan on July 5, 1955. A small press activist, he founded the Ibbetson Street Press (Somerville, Massachusetts) in 1998. Holder is a co-founder of The Somerville News Writers Festival and is the curator of the Newton Free Library Poetry Series, both in Massachusetts. His work has appeared in such magazines as *Rattle, Doubletake, The Boston Globe Magazine, Poesy, Small Press Review, Artword Quarterly, Manifold* (UK), *The Café Review, the new renaissance,* and many others. He holds an MA in Literature from Harvard University.

Colophon

The text is set in Monotype's Bodoni, which is based on cuts by the eighteenth century Italian master printer Giambattista Bodoni. This typeface was a breakthrough design widely credited with creating the modern letter style that places emphasis on mathematically vertical strokes.

The papers are Wausau Paper Royal Fiber Birch 70 lb text and Fox River EverGreen Hickory 80 lb cover. Both papers contain 30% post-consumer fibers; the Wausau paper is also Forest Stewardship Council certified.

Design by David McNamara.